RMS Queen M
50 Years of Splendour

Introduction

Queen Mary was more than one of the greatest ships ever built, carrying the rich and the famous between Southampton and New York at great speed. She was more than a prestigious mail-carrying symbol of the country and of the Company that brought her into being.

She represented a nation's hope when she was first designed and laid down; she represented a nation's disappointment when work on her ceased because of the depression; she represented a new hope when she was finally completed and launched, the ultimate achievement of the technology of the age. She represented the embodyment of many dreams.

Ever since her conception she has captured the imagination; ever since her disappearance from the waters of the North Atlantic she has continued to represent in her latter role at Long Beach, the popular ideal of an ocean liner.

In the year that marks the 50th anniversary of her maiden voyage this publication can only hope to celebrate, in some small way, the legend of the *Queen Mary*.

Commodore Geoffrey Marr summed up the impact that not only the *Queen Mary* but also her sister the *Queen Elizabeth* made when he quoted: 'The two *Queens* undoubtedly will always remain the finest ships ever built. They're talking about tankers of 500,000 tons but no tanker, no matter what its size, could ever convey the visual impact of these two magnificent ships, especially when seen at speed, flinging aside the North Atlantic in huge combers, the hull line one of power and splendour: oceanic palaces of magnificent proportions.'

Who could follow that.

David F. Hutchings
Fareham 1986

Dedication

To my late uncle William Way of Cowes, surveyor of lifeboats for the RNLI and an early influence on my love of ships and shipbuilding.

Courtesy, University of Liverpool Cunard Archives

© David F. Hutchings &
Kingfisher Publications
ISBN 0 946184 23 2
First Published June 1986
Second Impression August 1988
Third Impression January 1990

Typeset and Printed
in Great Britain

Contents

Cover: designed by David Hutchings with illustrations from a painting by Harley Crossley and the company motif from a Cunard ash-tray.
Inside front: a superb study of the *Queen Mary* in her element.
Captain John Treasure Jones collection
Back cover: a particularly good vantage point to watch the *Mary* leave Southampton was at Hythe, a superb photograph of her in mid July 1964 illustrates this.
K.L. Cook

Published by
Kingfisher Publications
65A The Avenue, Southampton SO1 2TA

Chapter One

Lifting the Cloud

Clydebank on Wednesday September 26th 1934 was grey, cold and very wet. In spite of that it was a special day, not only for the Clydesiders who were taking a specially declared public holiday, but for the whole of Britain.

After three years of the worst economic depression in world history the country was launching its biggest ship from the Clydeside shipyard of John Brown in the presence of their Majesties King George V, Queen Mary and HRH The Prince of Wales, the latter being there in his guise as Master of the Merchant Navy and Fishing Fleets.

Number 534, the shipyard number by which the new Cunard-White Star liner had been known for so long, was symbolical of the rebirth of a nation. Work on her had stopped a year after it had started and No. 534 had lain uncompleted and rusting on the stocks whilst Britain languished in the years of the Depression and the resulting mass unemployment.

When it was decided to recommence the building of No. 534 it seemed to represent the turning point in Britain's fortunes and her progress was followed with keen interest.

To mark this start of a return to normality the Queen had graciously consented to launch the giant liner and in doing so became the first reigning British monarch to perform such a

Umbrellas are lowered as the King and Queen acknowledge the cheering crowd prior to proceeding to the launching platform. 534 dominates the background 'lofty as a tower'.
Topical Press

ceremony. John Masefield, the Poet Laureate, had composed a special poem, entitled 'Number 534', to mark the occasion of the launch. It is here reproduced in full:

> For ages you were rock, far below light,
> Crushed, without shape, earth's unregarded bone.
> Then Man in all the marvel of his might,
> Quarried you out and burned you from the stone.
>
> Then, being pured to essence, you were nought
> But weight and hardness, body without nerve;
> Then Man in all the marvel of his thought,
> Smithied you into form of leap and curve;
>
> And took you, so, and bent you to his vast,
> Intense great world of passionate design,
> Curve after changing curving, braced and masst
> To stand all tumult that can tumble brine,
>
> And left you, this, a rampart of a ship,
> Long as a street and lofty as a tower,
> Ready to glide in thunder from the ship
> And shear the sea with majesty of power.
>
> I long to see you leaping to the urge
> Of the great engines, rolling as you go,
> Parting the seas sunder in a surge,
> Shredding a trackway like a mile of snow
>
> With all the wester streaming from your hull
> And all gear twanging shrilly as you race,
> And effortless above your stern a gull
> Leaning upon the blast and keeping place.
>
> May shipwreck and collision, fog and fire,
> Rock, shoal and other evils of the sea,
> Be kept from you; and may the heart's desire
> Of those who speed your launching come to be.

'....rolling as you go' and '....all gear twanging shrilly' foresaw with clarity two of the new liner's less amiable propensities.

By the afternoon of the launch day itself an estimated two hundred thousand people, at least, many paying fifteen shillings for a seat in specially constructed stands, converged onto the shipyard and into the fields on the banks of the Clyde, opposite to the shipyard. The river had been newly dredged over a length of 1800 ft from the slipway and had been widened to take the length of the ship.

The rain that had deadened the preceding and worrying wind continued but the mass of black umbrellas was lowered as the royal party, passing 'yards of ermine and gold braid' as one observer put it, ascended to the glass enclosed launching platform.

For the first time, too, the launching ceremony was being broadcast to an eager nation and after Sir Percy Bates, the Chairman of Cunard-White Star, had welcomed the royal guests the King made his speech:

'The sea with all her tempests, will not be readily bridled, and she is stronger than man; yet in recent times man has done much to make the struggle with her more equal.

Today we come to the happy task of sending on her way the stateliest ship now in being. I thank all those here and elsewhere whose efforts, however conspicuous or humble, have helped to build her. For three years her unaccomplished hull has lain in silence on the stocks. We know full well what misery a silent dockyard may spread among a seaport and with what courage that misery is endured. During those years when work upon her was suspended we grieved for what that suspension meant to thousands of our people.

We rejoice that, with the help of my Government, it has been possible to lift that cloud and to complete this ship. Now, with the hope of better trade on both sides of the Atlantic, let us look forward to her playing a great part in the revival of international commerce.

It has been the nation's will that she should be completed, and today we can send her forth, no longer a number on the books, but a ship with a name, into the world, alive with beauty, energy and strength.

Samuel Cunard built his ships to carry the mails between the two English-speaking countries. This one is built to carry the people of the two lands in great number to and fro so that they may learn to understand each other. Both are faced with similar problems and prosper and suffer together.

We send her to her elements for the good will of all the nations as a mark of our hope in the future. She has been built in fellowship among ourselves. May her life among great waters spread friendship among the nations.'

No. 534 presented a magnificent spectacle to passing commuters and sightseers alike.   *Harley Crossley collection*

The well-kept secret of No. 534's name is finally revealed as Her Majesty the Queen christens her *Queen Mary* from behind a rain-streaked window. *Courtesy, University of Liverpool Cunard Archives*

The complete launch took 100 seconds.
Southampton Maritime Museum

Some of the 2,350 tons of drag chain used to check the *Queen Mary's* speed once she was waterborne.
Courtesy, University of Liverpool Cunard Archives

The King's fine epithet '....the stateliest ship', was to remain with the ship during the ensuing years.

The Queen then stepped forward and, possibly forgetting that the launching was being broadcast, whispered 'Which buttons do I press?' She then made her eagerly awaited speech and in naming the ship ended years of popular speculation. Because of the well-kept secret the letters of the liner's name had not yet been riveted to the hull. Many suggestions had been put forward as possible contenders for No. 534's name – *Victoria, Britannia* and many others, usually with the – 'lA' suffix that had been given to the majority of Cunard ships in the past. However, because of the recent amalgamation between the Cunard and White Star Lines it was felt politic not to offend the White Star interests whose ships had traditionally used the suffix – 'lC' (*Britannic, Olympic, Majestic* etc) and the final choice pleased both shipping lines and the country as a whole.

'I am happy', the Queen spoke clearly making, this, her first public speech, 'to name this ship *Queen Mary.* I wish success to her and to all who sail in her.' Then, with a pair of golden scissors, the Queen cut a pink ribbon which sent a bottle of Australian wine arcing across the void between platform and ship to shatter its contents against the towering knife edge of the *Queen Mary's* bow. Her Majesty then turned to the King and asked, 'Was that right?'

The Queen then pressed the first of two electric buttons which set in motion the results of four years of complicated calculations and model experiments. Six triggers, that had been holding back the *Mary's* 35,500 ton launch weight on the inclined slipway, were released. The second button, when pressed, started six hydraulic rams that began to push the grey-painted ship backwards on her sliding cradle with an ever-increasing motion towards the Clyde.

As the liner's bow, still encased in its wooden and steel cradle (the 'fore-poppet'), dipped from the edge of the slipway into the river, 2,350 tons of drag chains, connected in bundles to various points along the giant hull, crashed and slid in clouds of rust after the liner, their great bulk and resistance gently bringing the *Queen Mary* to a halt. It had been calculated that the liner would, on this first and perhaps most critical journey of her career, travel 1,194 feet before being brought to a halt. In fact, she travelled just 2 feet more than calculated, a marvellous verification of the naval architect's art.

Spectators on the banks of the Clyde opposite to the shipyard had a magnificent view of the launching, even if some of them did get their feet wet!

Cyril Saunders collection

The ship had also needed a considerable amount of internal shoring to give her additional stiffness during the launch and hundreds of tons of steel girders and wooden shores had been erected inside her. To maintain strength in her superstructure the windows had not yet been cut along her promenade deck.

Between the 100 seconds of her first faltering movement to the time that she was brought to a halt the spectators had given her a tumultuous reception, even those who had tried to keep clear of the resulting flood-wave that hit the opposite shore. The ceremony and launch had lasted a mere fifteen minutes and on its completion the King and Queen descended the platform steps to meet the men who had built the 'Queen' and then to attend a reception in the shipyard's mould loft.

The 'Mary', herself, was gently towed to her fitting out berth in a strengthening wind that made the job increasingly more difficult. This berth would be her home for the next eighteen months whilst engines, boilers and many thousands of items that go to make an ocean liner were fitted.

Immediately after the launch the *Queen Mary* was carefully edged alongside her fitting-out berth. The wetness of the day can be judged from the jetty planking. The tug *Paladin* is to the right.
Courtesy, University of Liverpool Cunard Archives

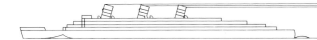

Chapter Two

A Dream Takes Form

The seeds of the idea that germinated into the *Queen Mary* had been sown in 1926 when a preliminary design for a long sought after thousand foot liner was sketched out in Cunard's design office.

Taking into account modern shipbuilding methods and materials, marine engines, types of fuel available (oil, coal or pulverised coal), numbers of passengers and classes to be carried, availability of building slips, dry-and wet-docking facilities etc, the designers had evolved a three-funnelled ship of fairly conventional appearance but with one advantage over all other existing ships – speed.

Later, in 1929, a Cunard committee began to seriously investigate a replacement (or replacements) for the ageing *Mauretania* of 1907, *Aquitania* of 1914 and the *Berengaria*, the latter having been the German liner *Imperator* of 1912 and taken over by Britain as part of the reparations after World War 1.

Until this time, three liners had been needed to maintain a weekly sailing between Britain and the United States but now two large, fast ships were being contemplated to provide the same regularity of sailings. 27½ knots was the minimum speed required to maintain this service, but a greater speed would be required to make up time lost through adverse weather conditions. An added factor would be one of prestige as such a pair of ships would be faster than the express ships of other nations and would attract the cream of the travelling public. Sir Percy Bates discounted any idea that the ships would be built to gain the coveted Blue Riband, saying that the ships being proposed would be the smallest and slowest ships that could provide the envisaged service.

After the initial idea had gone through several changes of design it was decided that a ship of nearly 1020 feet in length and with a beam of 118 feet would best be suited to the company's requirements. The choice of boilers had posed one particular problem but, eventually, water tube boilers gained preference over the originally proposed 'Scotch' boilers. This had upset the calculations of the ship designers as a lot of weight would be taken from low down in the hull where it was most needed to provide sufficient stability. A complete redesign was avoided, however,

when a new system of piping, using lighter pipe materials, was adopted in the higher realms of the ship, thus compensating for any weight lost below the waterline.

The contract for the first of the two new liners was awarded to the renowned John Brown shipyard on Clydeside and was executed on 1st December 1930. The ship was given a building number in the builders' books and became popularly known to the world by that number, 'No. 534', until the very day of her launch.

The keel of No. 534 was laid on 27th December and the first rivet was driven home by an ex-apprentice who had become the Shipyard Manager, Mr. Donald Skifflington.

For the following twelve months the ship grew in stature as frames were erected and plated and beams and decks were laid. Progress on the building proceeded well, so well, in fact, that Sir Percy Bates thought that the ship would be ready for launching in February 1932, four months ahead of schedule and thus be ready for sea by mid-1933. So, according to this estimation, the giant liner (at 73,000 tons – later revised to 83,000 tons – she was half as big again as the previous largest liner, the *Majestic*) was within five months of being ready for launching when a devastating blow fell 'like a bolt from the blue.'

The world had slid into a general economic recession that became known as The Depression but Cunard had been able to soldier on bravely through its early months, even managing to show a profit. It was then found that the available money was needed for insurances, depreciation of the existing fleet, maintaining services and that little or no money was available to complete No. 534 and to finish the ship would prove to be an unbearable burden on the company's resources. The liner had not been subsidised by the British government as it was not anticipated that she would be used in time of war, as had for example the *Lusitania* and *Mauretania* which had been built to Admiralty specifications.

The Cunard company therefore had no other choice than to suspend any further work on 534 and this suspension, coming into effect on Friday 11th December 1931, meant dismissal for 3,000 men who worked directly on the ship and to a further 6 to

One of the early proposals for the *Queen Mary's* design.

National Maritime Museum

7,000 more who were employed in various sub-contracting industries ranging from steel forgings to cutlery producers and from carpet weavers to potters. The cessation of work also symbolised the onslaught of the worst of the Depression to the people of a maritime nation who had followed the ships' construction with avid interest, feeding on all the superlatives that the contemporary press could offer.

Whilst the ship languished so did Britain and it was popularly believed, like the search for some holy grail, that as soon as the work restarted on 534 so would Britain find its way back to full employment and prosperity.

For 27 long, hard months the liner lay rusting on the stocks accumulating 130 tons of rust along with innumerable nests of birds that found the man-made cliffs of steel an ideal breeding place.

Smoke and mist hung in a pallid veil over the quiet, hungry town, the usual staccato rythms of rivetting silenced, a silence that spread its meaning of unemployment to all corners of the country.

But in one corner, in the chamber of the House of Commons, this silence was challenged. David Kirkwood, Labour Member of Parliament for Dumbarton Burghs, demanded the resumption of work on 534 to alleviate the unemployment in his constituency. He said 'I believe that as long as No. 534 lies like a

For 27 months No. 534 remained silently on the building slip collecting 130 tons of rust. *Shipbuilding and Shipping Record*

David Kirkwood, the Member of Parliament who did so much to get work restarted on No. 534. *Southampton Maritime Museum*

skeleton in my constituency so long will the depression last in this country. To me it seems to shout Failure! Failure! to the whole of Britain,....' At first, his cries went unheeded but gradually sympathetic ears listened to his pleas and took up his cause.

The problem was, how to finance the idea. The government refused to subsidise Cunard and Cunard could not afford to restart work from its own finances. After lengthy and complex discussions a solution was found and the government agreed to make Cunard a repayable loan under certain conditions.

The making of a loan to build an express ship was in itself most unusual in that all foreign competition to 534 had been built with state aid and had been, or would be, run with state subsidies, the ship's themselves being loss-makers for the sake of being prestigious. Not only would 534 be paid for from private capital (albeit via a loan) but would be run on a profit-making basis, making her unique amongst her contemporaries.

To add to the financial complexities of the government loan to Cunard it was stipulated, as part of the agreement, that the company should take over the ailing White Star Line as a running mate.

This steamship line had been founded in 1867 and had run many fast and famous ships in the late 19th century but had latterly built for size and comfort. In 1902 the Line had been purchased by the American owned International Mercantile Marine Company although the ships of the line remained under the British flag and with British crews (in case of requisition in

time of war). However, from 1927, the White Star Line once again became purely British when it was purchased by the Royal Mail Steam Packet Company, adding it to its vast empire of interwoven shipping companies under the chairmanship of Owen Phillips, Lord Kylsant. Because of the complexity of its financial arrangements RMSP found itself in difficulties and White Star was once again offered for sale. Cunard was interested but was dubious about the financial pitfalls that would accompany the purchase and the company 'backed-off'. The British government stepped in to champion White Star and made it a condition of the financial loan to Cunard that the two companies should merge. Thus came into being Cunard White Star Ltd., but Cunard consoled itself by the fact that they now had £9.5 million, – £3 million to complete 534, £1.5 million to provide working capital for the new company and a further £5 million for the construction of a long awaited sistership to the liner already under construction.

So, on Tuesday 3rd April 1934, four hundred men, led by two kilted pipers, marched through the jubilant streets of Clydeside back to the open gates of John Brown's Shipyard to start clearing the rust from the hull of No. 534. Formal notice to restart construction was received by the yard on 26th May and thus the campaigning of David Kirkwood M.P. along with the shrewd business acumen of Sir Percy Bates had brought about the impossible dream – the mammoth liner was to be completed. Clydeside was back at work and, taking heart from the renewed vigour in that one shipyard, Britain herself became revitalised.

Immediately after Easter 1934, men went triumphantly back to work led by pipers. *Shipbuilding and Shipping Record*

Chapter Three

The Wonder Ship

From the time of her conception the *Queen Mary* was planned to be the ship of the age – 'The Wonder Ship'. Everything about her was to be big both in quantity and quality and, without apology, this chapter sets out to list a few of the statistics and superlatives that made her 'The Big Ship'.

From the turn of the century the public, always thirsty for details of the glamorous big liners that plied their trade back and forth across the Atlantic, were supplied with comparisons as each new ship entered the lists.

Photographs, or artist's impressions made when a photograph was not possible, abounded depicting the current liner that was having its virtues extolled shown in most unlikely poses in order to give an idea of its size in comparison with famous buildings or landmarks. Upended against the Eiffel Tower or the Empire State Building, having locomotives driven through a cavernous funnel or seemingly to have run aground along one side of the Great Pyramid of Cheops, all served to astound the hopefully potential traveller who would be attracted to the biggest or the fastest ship of the day.

In this, the *Queen Mary* was no exception. One famous illustration showed the ship with her bows in Whitehall, her starboard bridge wing almost dislodging Nelson from his column in Trafalgar Square and her stern creating mayhem at the Coliseum theatre in St. Martin's Lane. The Londoners seeing this huge vessel blocking their streets do not seem to be over perturbed. Another sketch illustrated the ship with the top of her forward funnel as being four feet above the centre of the clock face at Westminster.

Although such visual clichés were commonplace to preceding generations that grew up when the liner was the only way to cross the oceans and carried the interesting, the rich, the famous, the notorious as well as the ordinary work-a-day folk, it is worth repeating some of the superlatives that caught the public's imagination when No. 534 was being built and came into service.

The first big item was her cost – £5 million. She was to be the first liner to be over 1,000 feet long, (the White Star had a thousand-footer on the stocks but this was cancelled and the French pipped the British at the post when their *Normandie* was finished before the *Mary* – she had been subsidised by the French government throughout the years of depression) she would be 1,019½ feet in overall length and her beam 118 feet. Her original gross tonnage was to have been 73,000 but this was later increased to 81,000. In the evolution of her hull design twenty two models, each almost 17 feet long, were made and with these eight thousand experiments were run in testing tanks, a total of one thousand miles being travelled.

The hull during construction on the stocks embodied 35,500 tons of steel by the time of launching, the stern frame alone weighing 190 tons and the rudder 180. Ten million rivets (4,000 tons) held the vessel together, the plates forming the hull and decks measured from 8 to 30 feet in length and weighed in from 3 cwt to 3 tons each. Painting the outer hull consumed 70,000 gallons of paint of which four coats of anti-corrosion paint was applied that it was hoped would last for forty years. Two thousand portholes and windows were cut into her sides and these used two and a half thousand square feet of thick, strengthened glass.

The liner had twelve decks and was divided into 160 watertight compartments.

The main features of the liner, her funnels, came under particular scrutiny. The distance from keel to the top of the forward funnel was 184 feet, was 30 feet in diameter and the distance between each funnel was 138 feet. The whistles, two on the fore and one on the middle funnel, were 6 feet 7 inches long

Typical of the artist's impressions of the day to convey the immensity of the ship, the *Queen Mary* brings London's traffic temporarily to a halt.
Courtesy W.H. Mitchell

No. 534 under construction showing some of the frames (or ribs) of the ship. *Southampton Maritime Museum*

One of the enormous castings that had to be moved from Darlington to Middlesborough before being shipped to the Clyde. The casting took the width of three railway tracks and the railway had to be closed for the weekend. It seemed as if all of Darlington turned out for the event.
Courtesy, University of Liverpool Cunard Archives

Lifeboats under construction at Hugh McLean and Sons Ltd. of Govan, Glasgow. Twenty-four lifeboats were carried and these could accommodate 3,266 people.
Courtesy, University of Liverpool Cunard Archives

The A-bracket casting that would take the propeller shafting constituted part of one of the strongest sections of the hull. This would later prove itself in practice in 1949.
Southampton Maritime Museum

One of the *Queen Mary's* four propellers. Each one was twenty feet in diameter and weighed 35 tons, 10 tons heavier than the previous largest that were fitted to the *Empress of Britain*.
Courtesy, University of Liverpool Cunard Archives

Above: Fitting-out the hull of *Queen Mary* is well underway. Windows have been cut into the superstructure along the promenade deck and scaffolding is ready to add the ships name at the stern.   *Cyril Saunders collection*

Left: A dramatic view of the *Queen Mary*.   C. Winchester, *Shipping Wonders of the World*

Below: As if supporting the name of her builders the *Mary* is well-advanced.
                    Courtesy, University of Liverpool Cunard Archives

Above: Three funnels fitted and painted in Cunard-White Star colours show that the liner is nearing completion.

Courtesy, University of Liverpool Cunard Archives

Below: The *Queen Mary* with one and a half funnels in place.

Shipbuilding and Shipping Record

and weighed one ton each. The beautiful, deep throated note (more like a roar!) that exuded from these whistles was said to be 'A, two octaves below the middle A on the piano'. However, even to the unmusical ear the sound produced never failed to thrill and could be heard at least ten miles away with the reverberations felt many times that distance away.

To propel the ship four 20 feet diameter, four bladed propellers, each costing £7000, were fitted. These were made from 50-ton 'Turbiston' castings which took fourteen days to cool. The final propellers each tipped the scales at 35 tons which made them the largest propellers made, to that date, by 10 tons.

The propellers were driven by four sets of quadruple expansion, reduced geared turbines, each having 257,000 blades, all hand set. Developing 50,000 horsepower they turned at 3,000 r.p.m., this speed being reduced to 200 r.p.m. at the propellers by a reduction gear that was itself 14 feet in diameter. The steam for the engines was provided by twenty four Yarrow-type water tube boilers, fuelled by oil from tanks holding 75,000 gallons, giving a working pressure of 400 pounds per square inch. Low-pressure steam for heating and cooking was provided by three double ended 'Scotch' boilers. Power to light the thirty thousand electric light bulbs, operate the twenty-two lifts, five hundred and ninety six clocks, etc, was supplied by seven turbo-generator sets that developed 10,000 kilowatts (enough to power a town of 150,000 people) and was distributed through the ship by four thousand miles of electric wiring!

The ship could be secured by the then largest anchors at 16 tons apiece, their cables (chains) of 165 fathoms (990 feet) a further 145 tons. The anchor cables, along with other cables and wire hawsers, would measure four miles if laid end to end!

For the safety of passengers and crew twenty four lifeboats would be carried, twenty of which were 36 feet long, 12 feet wide and each with a capacity for 145 people. These were built by Hugh McLean and Sons Ltd. of Glasgow.

Passengers carried were up to 776 cabin (first) class, 784 tourist (second) and 579 third. 1101 officers and crew looked after the safety and welfare of the ship and passengers.

After the heady statistics of the *Queen Mary's* construction, the shopping list for this incredible ship would make any land-based housewife quake:

Above: A splendid view of the cabin-class lounge which became the soci[...] centre of the liner. At its maximum height of 30 feet the room extend[...] through three decks. This room contained the Steinway piano which us[...] the main woods employed in the lounge, makoré and maple burr. The g[...] relief is by Maurice Lambert.

Left: The Observation Bar and Cocktail Bar is semicircular in plan, wit[...] upholstery of red-hide and panels of maple burr with bands of cedarwoo[...] The painting 'The Royal Jubilee Week 1935' above the bar is b[...] A.R. Thompson.

Right: Cabin-class Main Restaurant showing Macdonald Gill's decorative map along which a crystal model of the *Queen* would 'travel' indicating her position. Seating is for 815 persons.

Photos – courtesy of Cunard

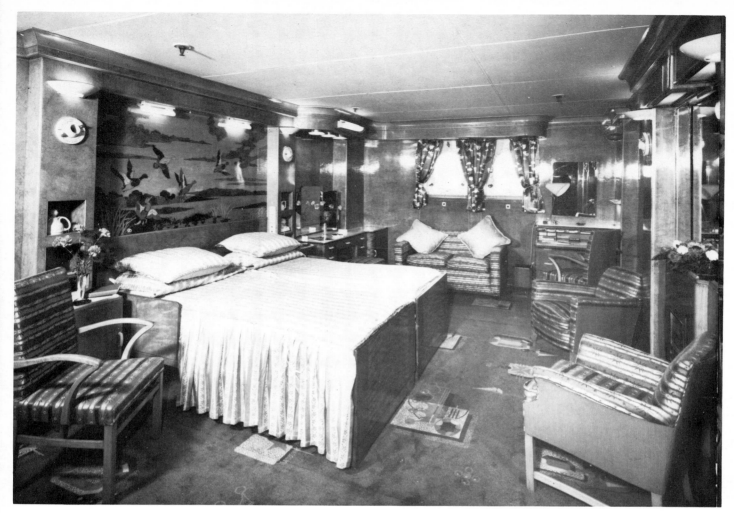

Ten thousand meals a day for four days had to be prepared but the catering staff could chose their menus from stores that included: 20 tons of fish, 20,000 lbs of poultry (chicken, duck etc.) 70,000 eggs, 3 tons of butter, 4,000 lbs of tea and coffee, 4,000 gallons of milk, 70 tons of meat (various!), 50,000 lbs of vegetables, not including 50,000 lbs of potatoes – 115,000 various bottles (including 20,000 of beer, 14,500 of wine and 5,000 of spirits), 2,000 lbs of cheese and 6,000 gallons of draught beer.

Although her vital statistics attracted some to travel in the *Mary* the details of her construction meant little to many of her passengers. It was 'chic' to travel in the biggest and fastest of ships but the interior decor of the liner also proved to be a great pull.

Again, more statistics but some which had more immediate appeal to the travelling public because these items surrounded the passengers for the four days of their voyage.

In the restaurants 16,000 items of silver plate were provided, including many pieces transferred from the old *Mauretania* when the latter was sold for scrap. To keep the passengers comfortable at night 30,000 sheets and 31,000 pillow cases had to be produced, altogether there was a half million items of linen. 200,000 pieces of earthenware, glass and china were on board and underfoot there was 6 miles of carpeting. For deck and cabin use 10 miles of blankets were made, for which 6,000 marino sheep unselfishly gave 16 tons of wool.

Since the advent of the French Line's *Ile De France* the decor of ocean liners had tended less to be copies of palaces or famous country mansions than to reflect, or even inspire, the tastes of the age into which they were launched. 534 was no

Above: Bedroom in cabin class reflected the luxury in which many travelled. The superb marquetry panel on the wall was typical of the fine workmanship employed throughout the liner.

Below: An artist's impression of a Tourist bedroom.

Courtesy, University of Liverpool Cunard Archives

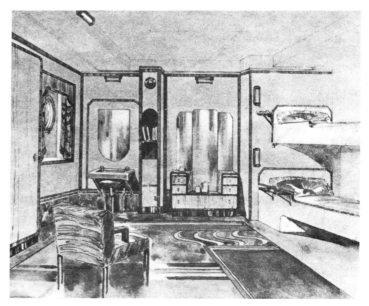

exception. In fact, to some commentators, she may have gone too far and her 'modernity' of the mid-30s had started to jade by the late 40s. But in her day she did set trends, starting a vogue of 'Ocean Liner' decor that could be seen in the Odeon cinemas with their curvilinear architecture, 'porthole' windows, ship-rail style bannisters on sweeping stairways and so on.

To panel the bulkheads and pillars over fifty types of wood were used for the veneering, some never having been used before. Woods were imported from all over the Empire, from Africa, Asia and America. Their very names conjured up exotic places, seemingly yet to be discovered. There were four types of ash, six of mahogany, four of oak, there was zebrano, rosewood, myrtle and satinwood, thuya, makoré, cedar and cherry and many, many more, all finished with a high degree of polish.

It is possible, within this short booklet, to describe only a few of the public rooms on board the *Mary* but the rooms that the veneers, mentioned above, adorned included one of the, if not *the*, largest room afloat. This was the Cabin Class Restaurant on 'C' deck, 143 feet long, extending the full width of the ship (118 feet) and 27 feet, maximum, in height. Other rooms included children's playrooms, a library, galleries, smoking rooms, drawing rooms, lounges, shops (W.H. Smith, Austin Reed and a souvenir shop), ballroom, the first synagogue afloat, and observation lounge with a gymnasium, squash court, swimming pool, turkish bath and 'frigidarium' amongst the facilities catering for the health conscious or those wishing to work off the extra pounds gained in the restaurants!

The cabin class lounge, 96 feet by 70 feet, with its 'autumnal gold' decor could be converted from the main first-class social gathering spot during the day to a ballroom at night simply by rolling back the huge Wilton carpet.

The aftermost deckhouse on the Sun Deck housed the elegant Verandah Grill with its black carpets, stylish murals and deep red, star-spangled curtains. This room was *the* place to be seen on *the* ship and to dine here would carry an additional charge.

Many of these rooms were adorned with original works of art especially commissioned by Cunard. Thirty six of the best contemporary British artists were invited to submit works, the *Mary* was not to be a museum ship! Sir Stanley Spencer declined

to prepare anything ('I only want to paint what *I* like and *not* what people want me to paint') and Duncan Grant's works were rejected by Cunard's chairman with a suggestion as to what the directors could do with them...... 'Give them to the blind school' was the retort!

Magnificent marquetry, designed by C. Cameron Baillie, adorned walls from third to first class; paintings by Kenneth Shoesmith graced the Roman Catholic altars in cabin and tourist classes ('Madonna of the Atlantic' and 'Madonna of the Tall Ships') as well as a beautiful group scene in the Cabin Class Drawing Room; various murals in metals by four sculptors – Messrs. Stanton, Lambert and the Gilbert brothers; Doris Zinkeisen's mural in the Verandah Grill; and Edward Wadsworth whose painting 'The Sea' contained symbolical allusions to that element complete with the *Queen Mary* appearing on the horizon and a pink ribbon draped around a central pillar: this ribbon should have been blue to represent the Blue Riband but the artist decided that there was too much blue on the ship and painted it pink.

For the forward bulkhead of the Cabin Class Restaurant Macdonald Gill designed a decorative and stylised (24 x 15 feet) map of the North Atlantic complete with a crystal model of the ship that moved to show the current position of the liner. At the opposite end of this room was a tapestry-style painting by Philip Conrad depicting English life and at the base of this hung a pair of finely worked bronze doors.

A marble plaque, designed by Lady Hilton Young, showing H.M. The Queen was hung in a panel of walnut burr and placed at the head of the main staircase facing the main hall and shops. Queen Mary's personal standard would also later be added in this vicinity.

In the Tourist Class Smoking Room there hung a magnificent painting by Charles Pears. This depicted the old *Mauretania*, smoke belching from her funnels and still painted in rust-streaked cruising white with masts cut down to pass under the Forth Bridge, en-route to the shipbreakers at Rosyth.

Thus an old Cunard favourite was shown sailing to her fate whilst the hull that carried her picture like a miniature of a departed loved-one was ready to sail at the beginning of her own reign of the Atlantic.

Amongst the shops on board W.H.Smith had a smart kiosk. Note the *Queen Mary* books in the window!

Courtesy, University of Liverpool Cunard Archives

Chapter Four

'...behold a city on th' inconstant billows...' Henry V, Act 3

The *Mary* continued her fitting-out alongside the jetty at John Brown's Shipyard and, because her stern extended some 100 feet beyond the end of the fitting-out berth and into the river, protective piles were driven into the bed of the Clyde to protect her from collision damage. These piles had previously been some of the interval stiffening beams used during her launch.

Other ships were still being built, of course, at the yard and launched. One vessel, the Anglo-American Oil Company's tanker *Comanche*, had an additional 480 tons of drag chains attached along her port side. Consequently, when she was launched the extra weight caused her to swing away from the *Mary* prior to dropping her anchors to prevent drift.

Other than attending the launching Edward, Prince of Wales, visited the ship twice whilst she was on the Clyde. Once at the instigation of David Kirkwood M.P. who urged him, whilst having a lengthy interview with the King, to visit the ship and town during the depression to see for himself the hardships being caused by the suspension of construction and, secondly, as King. To the grief of the nation, King George V, the 'Sailor King', had died on 21st January 1936 the Prince succeeding him as King Edward VIII and as such visited the ship for a lengthy tour of inspection on 5th March. The King upset the official tour that was planned by insisting on seeing, not only the first class areas that he was usually shown, but the crews' quarters and where they ate.

As the royal visitor and his entourage left the shipyard the siren of Britain's greatest liner sounded for the first time in salute to the King and Emperor of the world's greatest Empire.

During the period of fitting out thousands of sight-seers flocked to the opposite banks and along the shores of the confluence of the Clyde and Cart rivers to inspect recent progress. They saw the letters, two and a half feet high, of the liner's name being fixed to either side of the bow and to the stern; they saw the funnels being fitted one by one and they saw the hull being painted, superstructure white, the hull a gleaming black and the funnels in Cunard orange-red with black tops and bands, and the painting signalled another important step in the *Mary's* career – her departure from the care of those who had so skillfully and unsparingly built her with affection, interrupted by so much suffering.

As the day gradually approached on which the *Queen Mary* would leave her birthplace an excitement gripped the country.

The French Line had finished their mammoth liner, the *Normandie*, well before Cunard White Star had completed 534. Although the keel of the French ship had been laid down a month after that of the *Mary*, she had been finished earlier (due to the more far-sighted financial policy of the French government) and had made her record-breaking maiden voyage a year ahead of her British rival; and rivals they were. To start with, the *Normandie* was given an overall length (tip of bow to stern) of 1,030 feet as opposed to the 1,019.5 feet of the *Queen Mary*, but length overall was purely 'cosmetic' as such extra length could be built into almost any ship and was useful for publicity propaganda. The length that mattered, at least to designers, was waterline length or 'length between perpendiculars'. For the *Mary* this was

The finishing touches: the 2½ feet high letters of the ship's name are secured and painted whilst the sheer line is lined-in carefully prior to the hull being painted black.

Courtesy, University of Liverpool Cunard Archives

1,004 feet (making her the first true thousand-foot liner), for the *Normandie*, 962 feet. On her maiden crossing to New York, the *Normandie* had achieved the Blue Riband, that allegorical symbol of speed. What the British public wanted to know was: would the *Queen Mary* wrest the honour from her arch-rival on her own maiden voyage? Cunard would not purposely attempt to do so, Sir Percy Bates insisted, as the *Queen* would only use sufficient speed to maintain her tight schedule and, besides, Cunard was not interested either in speed records or in racing as the company had always put safety first.

Six weeks after King Edward's visit to the ship the *Queen Mary* was ready to sail. At 9.45 am, Tuesday 24 March 1936, four blasts from her mighty sirens boomed out across Clydebank to announce to one and all that she was ready to go. This was one hour earlier than expected due to a freshening wind which might cause problems as the liner attempted to navigate the bends in the river.

Over the previous weeks many thousands had travelled far just to see the liner fitting-out but for her departure schools had closed and a holiday had been declared. So, on this special day an estimated one million people had travelled by rail, motorbus, car, bicycle, foot, or by any other means, to line the banks of the Clyde to watch the sailing of that river's greatest creation – 'Britain's Masterpiece' as Cunard so aptly called her, the phoenix of Britain's ordeal by Depression.

Five tugs of the Clyde Shipping Board, the *Flying Falcon*, *Flying Kite*, *Flying Eagle*, *Flying Spray* and *Flying Foam*, were accompanied by the *Romsey*, that had come up from Southampton, and the locally based *Paladin*, a tug-tender belonging to the Anchor Line. The *Paladin* had been chosen to lead the *Mary* during her journey down the Clyde and would later be purchased by Red Funnel Steamers of Southampton, coming south ten years later in 1946 to join her massive charge.

Slowly, the great ship was lead astern into the Clyde and partly into the deepened river Cart before her head was turned downstream and seawards at around 7 knots.

The liner was under the joint command of Captains Duncan Cameron and John Murchie, two of the best known men in Clyde pilotage. The journey was fraught with tension and this reached a climax as the *Mary* approached a bend in the river near Dalmuir. A gust of wind caught the ship and swung her stern across the river so that her enormous length almost blocked the stream ('We skidded', said an unflurried Captain Cameron). Her stern was aground for several seconds until the tugs had her off, but during that brief period people on shore had chatted to those on board. The incident also got her an entry into the daily casualties list at Lloyds.

The crowds cheered her for the fifteen miles of her river passage until, at last, the Clyde widened and when the *Mary* with her gaggle of tugs arrived off Gourock she let go her anchors. This was to be one of many trials of her equipment that she was to carry out here including adjustments to her compass. She also took onboard her lifeboats. Only two had been carried as emergency boats during her journey from the shipyard and, also, neither had her furniture been loaded or had much fuel been taken on, all this was to reduce her draught as much as possible.

The *Queen* stayed for two nights off Gourock and each evening she was brilliantly lit all along her length through myriads of gleaming portholes and windows and, with her funnels floodlit, she provided an unforgettable spectacle to the thousands who viewed her from the shores or from pleasure craft splashing around her sparkling bulk.

Left: The triumphant day of departure. Thousands watched the *Mary's* sailing from the vantage point of fields opposite the shipyard. Agriculture and industry indelibly intertwined.
Courtesy, University of Liverpool Cunard Archives

Below: The *Mary's* stern is eased into the River Cart as her nose is manoeuvered seaward.
Cyril Saunders collection

Above: The Clyde swirling with the movement of ships as the *Mary* takes her first sea-steps.   *Cyril Saunders collection*

Above: Slow ahead the *Mary* is eased from her birthplace. The *Paladin* can be seen in her role as lead-ship. The Clyde had been specially dredged with millions of cubic feet of spoil being removed.   *Frank O. Braynard*

Right: Two fine views showing the *Mary's* stately progress down the Clyde.   *Cyril Saunders collection*

Anchored off Gourock with the Highlands behind her, the *Mary* prepares to take on her lifeboats.

Courtesy, University of Liverpool Cunard Archives

With a 'bone in her teeth' the *Mary* undergoes her trials.

Author's collection

By the early hours of the morning of the 26th the various trials had been completed so, at 2.30 am, she weighed anchor and set course for Southampton.

In Southampton preparations had been going on for years to receive the *Queen*. At first it seemed as if the town would not become the British port for the liner as the Southern Railway Company, under the chairmanship of Sir Herbert Walker, was reluctant to build a £1.85 million dry dock that was big enough to accommodate a ship that would only use it perhaps twice a year, bringing in, at the most, £10,000 in dues. In the end, Sir Percy Bates, told the railway company 'No dock, no ship!' and intimated that either Liverpool would become the home port or else Cunard would build its own port on the South Coast in rivalry to Southampton.

His subtle blackmail worked, Southern Railway relented and the 1,200 foot long King George V dry dock was built. The dock, at the northern end of a vast new dock area built entirely on reclaimed land, was officially opened on 26th July 1933 by the King and Queen who sailed into the huge new basin on board the Royal Yacht *Victoria and Albert*.

The populace around the southern shore were as excited at the prospect of receiving the 'Stateliest Ship Now In Being' as the Clydesiders had been in building her. Local newspapers had been publishing features about the vessel for weeks ahead and by Friday 27th March thousands from all over Hampshire, the Isle of Wight and beyond, prepared to make the day a holiday, flocking to line the shores of Spithead, the Solent and Southampton Water.

The liner, it was reported, had touched 29.3 knots on a short spurt, without being pressed, during her trip from the Clyde.

Hundreds of items had been produced to foster the public's interest in the liner. *Queen Mary* berets featured a profile of the liner on the top of the hat; chocolate *Queen Marys*; *Queen Mary* jig-saws; magazines, booklets and pamphlets; a *Queen Mary* board game where small models of the ship were raced around Britain at the shake of a dice; models and give-away photographs of the liner were amongst the souvenirs to whet, but seemingly never to satiate, the appetite of the public.

The *Queen Mary* arrived in majesty to anchor off Cowes at 7 am on Friday 27th (many of the important dates in her career seemed to feature the 27th!) and she was to remain there until midday, private vessels and paddle steamers sloshing around her during her stay there, with aeroplanes circling her Gulliver-like form in the sky overhead, awaiting the next high tide.

By noon an estimated three quarters of a million people had amassed onto the surrounding shorelines to witness her regal procession from the Solent up Southampton Water to Southampton itself. Pilots Captain Wallace Caws then Captain George Bowyer had taken charge of the *Mary* during, this, her first arrival in the South.

She sailed past the outward-bound German liner *Bremen* (an ex-Blue Riband holder), dressed overall with code flags and also flying the Swastika. (Many passengers would eventually take their patronage from the German liners with their Nazi overtones to join the sparkling new *Queen*). The captain of the *Bremen* signalled: 'Our heartiest congratulations for the completion of our youngest and biggest companion at sea. May our first meeting be the beginning of a long, good co-operation. Commodore Ziegebein, Officers and Crew'.

Arriving in the south for the first time, the *Mary* passes the German liners *Bremen* and *Hamburg*.   *Frank O. Braynard*

The *Queen Mary* arriving at Southampton for the first time with thousands watching her arrive. Here she is passing the Union Castle liner *Windsor Castle* and White Star's *Majestic*.

Cyril Saunders collection

The brotherhood of the sea was at work and any idea of what was to happen to that 'long, good co-operation' was still a distant dot on the horizon of world history. Captain Sir Edgar Britten made reply:

'Please accept from myself, officers and crew our warmest appreciation of your kind message. The *Queen Mary* will, we all feel sure, be a worthy successor of those fine ships which have preceded her in the waters of the North Atlantic and of which your noble vessel is one of the brightest examples. Kindest greetings.'

Hundreds of craft surrounded the *Mary* as she approached Southampton Docks with ferries and pleasure craft carrying thousands to view the liner close to. Twelve thousand people were in the Southern Railway's docks as well as thousands more who saw her from the shore.

Greetings were sounded from the liners berthed in the Eastern Docks, and in the Western Docks (the new 7,000 feet of docks completed on the reclaimed Millbrook Bay) she passed by the four-funnelled *Windsor Castle* and the *Majestic* (once a White Star liner and now awaiting sale and possible scrapping. She did,

An anxious trial as the *Queen* enters Southern Railway's King George V dry dock. The old White Star liner *Majestic* can be seen on the left. Donald MacLean (later Commodore of the Cunard Line) was watching from her bridge.

Courtesy, University of Liverpool Cunard Archives

so each man knew where to go and what to do when he arrived on board. The ship was also divided into 'Red', 'White' and 'Blue' sections and a soldier would be punished with extra duties if he trespassed into the wrong section. On leaving New York with thousands of men on board the *Mary* was in special peril. With the additional weight of human cargo she drew an extra 2 feet of water and the men were ordered to stand still in their quarters whilst the ship left harbour. If they had been tempted to rush to wave farewell to the Statue of Liberty then the ship would have listed at least 10° and would have increased her draught on the 'deep' side by 4 feet. This would have been enough to rupture the sub-river tunnels beneath the Hudson.

As the troops travelled they indulged themselves in several activities which were not to Cunard's or the authorities' liking – amongst these were playing dice ('craps' was a great favourite) and as far as the ship's company was concerned the chewing of gum was unpopular – it was difficult to clean off bulkheads and decks – as was the carving of initials in the teak-wood handrails. The latter was eventually tolerated and as Captain Bisset later wrote '......I decided not to make a fuss about this. These men might soon be going into battle, and some of them would never return to their homes and loved ones. Let them amuse themselves!' These carvings would later become treasured relics.

To the American soldiers, the *Queens* were so huge that they believed that only the United States could have built them!

Amongst the celebrities who travelled on board the liner during the war one in particular should be mentioned. This was a gentleman who travelled under the pseudonym of 'Colonel Warden'. He travelled three times on the *Mary*, partly because of being affected by tuberculosis at one time which prevented him from using aircraft. He always travelled with a large retinue and used the chance of sailing in the Cunarder to make several important decisions. The *Mary* would wait for him (at one time for eighteen days) to rejoin her and he was always appreciative of her crew and qualities and even cabins were especially refurbished for his use. The man in question was Winston Churchill.

During the war HRH Queen Mary did not forget the ship that bore her name and messages were exchanged between the two. One in particular was sent by Her Majesty from her shelter in the country just before D-Day:

'Since I launched the *Queen Mary* nearly ten years ago, almost half of her life has been spent on active war service. Now, as the war enters upon this decisive phase, I send my warm greetings to the Captain, Officers and the Ship's Company, and to all those who sail in the ship that bears my name.
It is always a source of pride and of pleasure to me to receive news of the magnificent work the *Queen Mary* is doing in the transport of troops from every quarter of the Empire and Commonwealth, and from the United States of America, to the theatres of war. I pray that before very long it may be her joyful duty to carry the victorious soldiers of the United Nations back to their homes and families in many parts of the world.
My earnest hope is that the many friendships born on board the *Queen Mary* during the years of war will continue into the happier years of peace to come, and that she will always prove herself a strong link, and a messenger of goodwill between the great English-speaking Nations.'

The Queen's speech reflected and qualified some of the statements made in her husband's, the late King George V's, speech at the launching ceremony of No. 534 ten years previously and her sentiment '......may be her joyful duty to carry the victorious soldiers...... back to their homes......' would soon be realised. When the *Mary* arrived in New York on 4th April 1945 she was laid-up for several weeks and dry-docked until it was decided that she would no longer be needed to transport American soldiers to Europe.

VE (Victory in Europe) Day was celebrated in the States,

Lifejackets were to be worn at all times! During a calm, summer crossing the troops could get some fresh air on the *Mary's* upper decks, although not much room was left for exercise!   *Imperial War Museum*

The *Mary* alongside the quay of the Ocean Dock, Southampton, on 27th December 1945.   *Author's collection*

as elsewhere, after the German collapse on 7th May and by this time both the *Mary* and *Elizabeth* were in New York and they joined in the port's armistice celebrations by adding to the crescendo of sound with their beautiful sirens.

The *Mary* did several more trips to Gourock but this time the numbers of eastbound passengers were low but westbound the numbers reflected the huge numbers of troops previously carried, but this time they were going home. With 14,777 G.I.'s on board the liner had a tremendous reception in New York with aircraft, boats, bands and crowds cheering her in. It was, at the time, the largest contingent of soldiers to enter the port on one ship and the *Mary* had also had the honour of taking the first U.S. units home.

During the war years the *Mary* had carried 810,730 passengers and steamed 661,771 miles. Winston Churchill felt that the *Queens* contribution to the war effort had shortened the conflict by a year and in his tribute to both of the *Queens* he said:

'Built for the arts of peace and to link the Old World with the New, the *Queens* have challenged the fury of Hitlerism in the Battle of the Atlantic. At a speed never before realised in war they carried over a million men to defend the liberties of civilisation. Often, whole divisions at a time were moved by each ship...... To the men who contributed to the success of our operations in the years of peril...... the world owes a debt that it will not be easy to measure.'

An impressive view showing the splendour of a liner at speed. The *Mary* has had her funnels repainted in Cunard colours but still retains her degaussing belt.

Courtesy, University of Liverpool Cunard Archives

The beauty of steam on land and at sea is combined in this splendid study taken at the docks in Southampton, April 1946. A boat train leaves behind Southern Railway 'N15' class No. 739 *King Leodegrance*.

Cyril Saunders collection

Zig-zagging and blackouts ceased and on Saturday 11th August 1945 the *Queen Mary* made her first post-war return to Southampton, again watched by thousands, berthing at 2pm accompanied by aeroplanes and boats, with the Southampton Police Band and civic dignitaries welcoming her back.

The *Queen Elizabeth* was the first Cunarder to be released from war work on 6th March 1946 whilst the *Mary* continued to repatriate American troops and the 'G.I. Brides', British girls who had married American servicemen and also girls who had married Canadians (the latters' wives were taken to Halifax, Nova Scotia). In all the *Queen* carried 30% of all the service wives, numbering 9,118 women and 3,768 children. Special facilities had been installed on board and an attempt, during a dry-docking, had been made to try and return the *Mary* to some sort of pre-war standard. Standee bunks, armour etc. were removed and by now the funnels had been painted in the cheery Cunard White Star colours.

The *Mary* was finally 'demobilised' on her return to Southampton on 29th September 1946 to begin a ten month refit. Ten thousand items of furniture had to be brought from storage from the New Forest, Australia and New York where they had been sent ashore in the early part of the war for safe keeping. These had to be renovated and collated and this was done at Ford's which had huge sheds at Eastleigh near Southampton. A new stem was fitted, degaussing strips and their protective steel shielding removed from around the sheer line, murals renovated and a thousand other tasks had to be completed to get the ship ready for sea. Men came from the Clyde to work on the liner and 120 lady french polishers were employed.

Above: On 29th September 1946 the *Queen* arrived at Southampton prior to being renovated for peacetime work. The *Queen Elizabeth* has already been refurbished and is ready to sail for New York.
Courtesy, University of Liverpool Cunard Archives

Below: The *Mary*, photographed on 5th April 1947, casts off her make-up of war. The degaussing strip had been removed as each square foot of her is repainted.
S.W. Baker

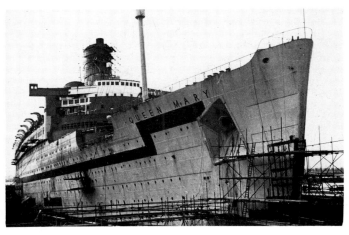

Friday 26th July 1947 and the *Queen Mary* arrives in the Solent after a short trials cruise. The *Queen Elizabeth* passes her off Cowes with an exchange of blasts from their sirens.
Illustrated London News

During the refurbishment the *Mary* benefited from experience gained from the *Elizabeth*. She had two garden lounges built on either side of the First Class smoke room, a permanent cinema converted from the starboard gallery on the Promenade Deck, a cocktail bar now greeted passengers in the entrance to the Main Restaurant and the gymnasium was moved to amidships on the Sun Deck. Tourist Class now had their own self-contained section of the Sports Deck between the first and second funnels and the crew had new accommodation. To aid in the navigation of the ship 'Seascan' radar was also fitted.

The *Queen Mary* was reconditioned by John Brown, her builders, as the main contractor and J. Thornycroft of Southampton was the main sub-contractor. Fifteen hundred men from Clydeside camped at Chandler's Ford and were taken each day to the liner. When the *Mary* was dry-docked her propellers were removed, her shafts drawn out for inspection and her underwater hull was scaled and coated with 3,000 gallons of anti-fouling paint.

When the *Mary* had returned to Southampton at the commencement of her refurbishing she had passed the *Elizabeth*, newly refitted, pristinely painted and ready for her own, long delayed commercial maiden voyage.

Sir Percy Bates had sadly died on the very eve of the *Queen Elizabeth's* maiden voyage which took place on 16th October and was thus denied the chance of seeing the realisation of the concept which he had supported and fought for so long ago – the two ship, weekly express service across the Atlantic.

By mid-July the *Mary* was ready to re-establish herself on her intended route and she was well booked for her post-war début.

The week before she sailed for New York she combined a trials trip to test her services with a short cruise, so on Thursday 25th July she left Southampton with 700 guests on board.

She returned the next day but anchored in Cowes Roads whilst the *Queen Elizabeth* sailed by, the two mammoth liners exchanging greetings. The *Mary* then entered Southampton Docks, occupying the berth recently vacated by her newer sister.

She sailed for New York on the following Thursday with 2,000 passengers. The *Queens* had at last laid claim to their rightful domain and together they would rule it in splendour for the next eleven years.

Chapter Six

Perils and People

In spite of numerous model experiments that had shown the *Mary* would be steady in almost any sea-state, she proved her confident forecasters, like the lady she was, to be presumptively wrong. She rolled badly. The crew would even come to say that she could roll the milk out of a cup of tea!

When she had appeared fresh and untried from her builders she had not even been fitted with safety storm rails along her corridors, such was Cunard's errant confidence in her. After a few voyages that had involved rough weather – and not a few injuries that brought ambulances to the quayside to meet her – workmen travelled on the ship to discreetly fit the missing safety rails.

One particular traveller during the war was obviously greatly influenced by the rolling liner. The traveller was Paul Gallico and it was he who was to later write a novel, *'The Poseidon Adventure'*, about a badly rolling liner that capsizes after being hit by a tidal wave. The book was later made into a film with a model of the *Queen Mary* starring as the *S.S. Poseidon*.

One famous statesman arriving in New York after a particularly rough crossing on the *Mary* was met by a bevy of news cameramen who had congregated at the Pier to meet him. But when they saw the storm damage to the *Queen*, – bent stanchions, crushed ventilators, ladders carried away, broken windows etc – their cameras were directed towards the ship.

The crew did not complain that their quarters had also been flooded. They just got on with the job and repaired the damage as best as they could until more permanent repairs could be made at a later date.

The insurance companies complained about the *Mary*, especially in the winter months. Broken crockery, furniture and peoples' legs caused the insurers to double their premiums and if this wasn't enough for Cunard, female passengers increasingly declined to travel on the liner in winter, especially as aircraft could provide an equally uncomfortable but quicker passage. Women were terrified of the ship in rough weather, so as a trial the shipping company had stabilisers fitted to their new *Media* in February 1952. To everyones' consternation the *Media* started to roll quite happily during the experimental voyage and obviously the stabilisers were not working as they should. When the liner arrived in New York a diver was sent down to inspect them and the reason why the ship had rolled so badly soon became apparent – the stabilisers had simply disappeared!

However, undaunted, Cunard had stabilisers fitted to the *Queen Elizabeth* but the officers of the *Mary* thought that their ship would never allow herself to succumb to such trickery.

Sir William Denny, the inventor of the stabiliser, travelled on the ship to observe her motion and he talked to the officers in the Engineers' Ward Room. He even demonstrated his ideas, with the aid of scale models, showing where he would fit two pairs of stabilisers to the ship to reduce its rolling.

Work was started on fitting the Denny-Brown stabilisers in 1957 and a few months and half-a-million pounds later the work was completed in 1958. The modification was a success and a roll of 10 degrees could be dampened to a fraction within seconds. The ladies, reassured by leaflets headed 'To Smooth Your Way Across the Atlantic', soon returned to the *Mary* whose roll was now almost a thing of the past except at high speed when the effect of the stabilisers was lessened.

Almost a thing of the past but not quite: In the autumn of 1964 the *Queen Mary* sailed from New York. The American meteorological office had forecast a typhoon and the liner's course supposedly took her well clear of it. Unfortunately, the typhoon had inconsiderately veered off its predicted course and, about two in the morning, struck without warning.

The Bridge had no time, or failed, to notify the Engine Room that trouble was imminent when the ship was suddenly caught in the vicious onslaught of a strong and continuous wind. As the liner was on her second day out from port she had settled down to her normal, fairweather, engine room routine. Amongst the calm-weather procedures one of the two turbo-feed pumps in each engine room had been switched off. These pumps maintained a pressure of feed water that kept the boilers 'topped-up' from either side and during moderate weather only two pumps were necessary to maintain feed to the boilers.

But when the typhoon struck the *Mary* listed 20° to starboard and was held there by the force of the wind. As a result, the boilers tilted with the ship and water went to one side of the boiler top drums whilst leaving the port side low. The automatic, or 'robot', valves controlling the feed-water levels detected this happening on each of the 24 boiler top drums (12 each port and starboard) and the starboard valves stopped feeding water which was perfectly acceptable. But the port side level was still low due to the continuing list and demanded more water (despite unrequired water on the starboard side still being available) which put an additional strain on the two operating feed pumps. In their efforts to supply water the pumps came close to

Leaflets enclosed with brochures extolled the virtues of the Denny-Brown stabilisers fitted to the *Queens*. The operating machinery on the *Mary* was fitted vertically due to space limitations. *Cunard*

Above left and right: The 'eyes and feet' of the liner were the Bridge and Engine Room, linked by the telegraph signals with their distinctive changing levers.

Courtesy, University of Liverpool Cunard Archives

overspeeding and tripping the turbo governors. The feed water pressure fell to just above the boiler steaming pressure: if the two needles indicating both pressures met and then suddenly passed each other it would be only a matter of seconds before the boilers melted down and blew.

The Boiler Room engineers watched the convergence of the needles and could only stand by, terrified. For some, prayer seemed to be the only solution.

By now the Bridge had got control of the situation and had turned the *Mary's* head into the wind and as the list decreased the water pressures normalised just as the Engine Room engineers had got the other two turbo-feed pumps into operation.

In the wake of the night's events the morning brought its own aftermath. A bright but turbulent dawn broke as a few passengers and crew ventured out onto the still heaving deck. An elderly lady passenger fell and injured herself as the *Mary* continued to roll. Looking over the ship's side the stabilisers could be seen as they were rolled out of the water by the *Mary's* motion, indicating the severity of the swell.

A dismal sight greeted an engineer when he returned to his cabin in the Engineers' quarters that had been built above the Verandah Grill shortly after the maiden voyage. The force of the gale had completely torn a steel-window cover away from its housing and another hung precariously from one hinge. To another engineer, 'Jack' Horner, an even more serious disaster had only just been averted:

He had left a bottle of whisky on the shelf above his wash basin and this, due to the rolling of the ship, had jumped over the fiddley surrounding the shelf, fallen through the sink (leaving a neat round hole in its wake) and had ended up – unbroken – on the cabin floor, there to be rescued with the aid of glasses from any other provocation of fate by the engineer and his friends.

Fog, too, presented a great danger to the ship even after she had been fitted with radar. Bad seamanship on the part of other vessels was always something to contend with so during fog extra lookouts were posted on the bridge wings, watertight doors closed and the Engine Room put on 'Stand By'.

The *Mary* would especially reduce speed to around 20 knots when, on her westward crossing, she crossed the 100 fathom line which indicated the edge of the Newfoundland Banks and the great possibility of meeting fishing boats. In years gone by many fishing vessels had gone missing, unreported by the fast ships that had possibly – perhaps unknowingly in light of the *Curacoa* incident – run them down. If another vessel's siren could be heard in the fog the *Queen* would veer away at 45° from the siren's direction for ten minutes before resuming course. But one particular problem had been foreseen in John Masefield's poem 'No. 534'

'......and all gear twanging shrilly as you race......'

for when the captain and senior officer on watch listened out for other ship's sirens from their posts on the *Mary's* bridge wings during fog they fought a losing battle. A ship's siren should be able to be heard from many miles away but this distance was reduced to a mile (thus decreasing the *Queen's* ability to manoeuvre in time) due to the interference of the whistling created by the *Mary's* own rigging.

As in any township the *Mary* contained within her walls the extremes of human emotions – birth and death.

For the latter, allied soldiers and prisoners-of-war suffered the ultimate pain when they succumbed to heat exhaustion when the *Mary*, during her trooping days, voyaged in the Indian Ocean and especially into the Red Sea.

And in the normal sailing days of peacetime her company was not immune from accidental death. One crew-member fell down a funnel, whilst a young third officer, Marshall, was found dead with a fractured neck at the bottom of the officers' stairway in 1948. It was supposed that he had turned to look at the clock at the top of the stairs whilst he was rushing to get ashore in New York, missed his footing and fell.

Burials at sea also took place with the ashes of former crew-members being committed to the deep.

On one such occasion, a greaser, having been told to empty a gash-can over the side noticed an officer gloomily and reproachfully looking at him. Later, the officer telephoned the engineer who had given the instruction to empty the can: 'Did he realise', the officer asked 'that the ashes of a deceased crew member had been committed to the deep just before the gash from the engine-room had been sent to join him?'

To redress the balance of death on board, the *Mary* also acted as a maternity ward to babes who became known as '*Queen Mary* citizens'. As is sometimes the case, a child born on a ship will take that vessel's name as his (or her) own, but when twin daughters were born on the *Mary* (one name solved) the dilemma of the other child's name was resolved by christening her *Elizabeth*.

The *Mary* also saved life and on more than one occasion sailors had the giant liner, her crew and medical staff to thank for their salvation. Even her presence gave ships in danger a feeling of security when they saw the *Mary* steaming towards them.

Unfortunately the *Mary* was also once 'duped'. A radio call informed the Captain, Commodore George Morris, that the skipper of a Greek ship was ill and that his symptoms were bad. The ship turned around and found the vessel with the 'injured' skipper at around two in the morning. There was blood all around the Greek skipper's cabin and he was taken on board the Cunarder. Once the liner was underway, the skipper made a remarkable recovery, probably aided by a suitcase full of money that he had brought with him. This episode had cost Cunard £5,000 and the *Queen Mary* twelve hours extra steaming.

The 'Big Ship' herself was endangered more than once. The first major occasion was when the liner had unhappily cut down and sank *HMS Curacoa* in the Second World War. Depth charges on the stricken cruiser could well have exploded as the naval ship sank around the *Queen*.

The second such occasion occurred on New Year's Day in 1949, although only briefly reported, or not mentioned at all, in the press and in subsequent biographies of the ship, it greatly affected the captain and officers of the liner who were the main participants in the drama. This has been borne out in subsequently published autobiographies and later reminiscences recalled in personal conversation:

The *Queen* was due to sail from Southampton on New Year's Day 1949 and blustery squalls were blowing in from the direction of the New Forest to the west. The *Mary's* Captain, Harry Grattidge, had only taken over the command of the liner three days before and to him fell the awesome responsibility to decide whether to sail in such weather. Around 1 in the afternoon there was a lull in the gales and, as tugs were available, the captain decided to leave with Jack Holt, the pilot, taking over the ship as far as the Nab Tower.

Picking up the French pilot, off the Brittany coast, the ship's company were reassured that the coast would provide some shelter. In order to pick up passengers arriving from Paris, there being no suitable overnight accommodation for them in Cherbourg the captain decided to enter Cherbourg Harbour, always difficult and still wrecked after the war, and anchor at 6.30 on that dark evening. Both anchors were dropped in the outer harbour.

The westerly wind had now changed to west-south-westerly, gale force 6 to 7 and by 8 pm the passengers were on board. The captain ordered 'All hands to stations' and for the ship to get underway. The anchors, held taut by the force of the wind, were taken in and as the port anchor was housed safely the pilot, Guy Frielaut, ordered the engines slow ahead. Then the starboard anchor came into sight clutching a long, black, shiny object in its flukes. 'Oh, look! There's a sea serpent on it!' a crew member was heard to call.

Pull as the captain might, the anchor could not get free of this obstacle and the pilot ordered full astern on both engines to ease the strain on the cable but still the anchor held fast. The wind increased in intensity and squalls blotted out the working party on the bow under the direction of Chief Officer Marr, who found it increasingly difficult to communicate with the bridge over the noise of the wind.

The recalcitrant anchor was once again let go, engine

A shipboard study of Commodore Geoffrey Thrippleton Marr, one-time officer and later captain of the *Queen Mary*.
R. Bruce Grice

manoeuvres executed and again an attempt was made to weigh the starboard anchor.

This time the anchor had two or three of the black lines on it and these, it was realised, were the remains of 'Pluto', the Pipe Line Under The Ocean, that had delivered petrol to the allied invasion forces in France. Unsuccessfully, Geoffery Marr tried to report to the bridge but heard the captain say 'Tell the Chief Officer there is nothing we can do for him now!' The port anchor was dropped as the *Mary*, continuing her astern drift, just missed rocks near the breakwater.

By now the captain had said, 'All right, Pilot, I'll take over', as tugs that had been signalled for had not appeared and the ship was still held by the tentacles of the pipeline on her dragging anchors.

At 9 pm there was a gentle bump and the liner stopped. An attempt with the engines did not move her and a signal was at once sent for tugs which yet again did not appear. The liner was obviously aground.

Low water was in half an hour and plans were made to transfer oil to barges and to get the passengers ashore to reduce draught as Geoffery Marr and his men got busy with flame torches to cut the ship free of the pipelines grip. Ultimately the passengers remained on board and much of the oil was transferred to other tanks.

The *Mary* had grounded at the western side of Cherbourg Harbour on a pinnacle of hard sand only a few feet wide called the Seleine Bank. By now the pilot, chain smoking and frantic, told the captain that at low tide the *Mary* would break her back. But, perhaps luckily, the liner had grounded on one of the few strong parts of her keel – between the two forward propellers.

By seven the next morning, after a night of hacking and burning, the pipeline was finally cut away. By now the four propellers could be seen as the tide had supposedly dropped by seventeen feet. Staff Officer (later Commodore) MacLean was to say years later that he had been told that the drop in tide was more like 21 feet!

The next high tide was due at 9.30 am but by 8 the *Mary* was afloat. She went astern out of the harbour, returned to the Solent where she anchored before returning to Southampton for dry-docking and inspection. A few rivets were found to be leaking and the keel was slightly concaved in the area of grounding. With difficulty sixty tons of cement was poured around the dent inside the ship and three days later the *Mary* continued her broken voyage to New York. Of the 1,700 passengers on board only three had decided to continue their journey by air. Dame Myra Hess and Benno Moiseiwitsch, the pianists, who were on board, entertained the passengers and many took the chance to explore the ship more fully in what turned out to be a ten day journey.

Perhaps, fortunately, the hours of darkness, that had covered the period of grounding and refloating and the appallingly bad weather had deterred any curious news photographers.

Other perils to the *Mary* were man-made, especially the times when she had to be docked in New York without the aid of tugs due to local strikes. This happened, firstly, before the war in 1938 when Commodore Sir Robert Irving, the Laird of Bonshawe, took her in and again in 1953 when the diminutive but highly respected Captain Donald Sorrell ('He had to stand on a box on the bridge!') took her in using a home-made sighting device previously constructed for use should such an event occur. At such times the *Queen* would wait for slack water, use the knuckle of Pier 90 as a pivot and pull herself in on her hawsers, previously landed by ship's boats. A very difficult and precise operation that brought telegrams of congratulations and herds of press – photographers hoping for a major crash that would interest their readers. Captain Irving's action actually broke the tugmens' strike.

Over the years of the *Queen Mary's* seagoing career many hundreds of people worked in her. Many famous passengers asked for their favourite steward, etc, to look after them during a voyage and this loyalty was repaid in many ways with holidays or medical bills for the crew-member being paid for by the well-attended passenger. From commis-waiter to officer, all of these people have often fascinating stories to tell and a picture gradually grows of what life was like on board an ocean liner.

Due to space limitations only two stories can be told of the many varied duties performed by the crew.

The day of a young commis-waiter such as Edwin Praine who had joined the *Empress of Britain* as a bell-boy at the age of 14 in 1932, on the maiden voyage in 1936, began when he woke at 5 am ready for a 5.30 start. His first duty was to collect a bucket of water and a pair of 'kneelers' and scrub the linoleum in the

Above: The damaged keel plates of the *Mary* after grounding on the table-sized Seleine Bank in Cherbourg Harbour.

Below: The damaged plates cut out and dumped on the side of the King George V Graving Dock, Southampton. November 1949.
Both National Maritime Museum

companionways. At 7.30 there was muster for a clean hands inspection prior to laying tables and then serving breakfast in the Main Restaurant, with long, white, starched continental aprons being worn. Breakfast finished at 10 am so a change of clothes was necessary either to serve lunch or to clean silver or portholes. Lunch continued until 2.30 pm and afternoon teas were served every other afternoon in the lounge. Alternate afternoons Edwin Praine had free unless, as a punishment for being late, portholes had to be cleaned. Dinner was served until 10 pm and the young waiter came off duty at 11 pm, tired out but ready to start, once again, next morning at 5 am!

Peter Jackson (later to captain the *Queen Elizabeth 2* on her journey to South Georgia during the Falklands war of 1982) joined the *Queen Mary* in November 1948 as Junior Third Officer having just obtained his Master's Certificate. Everything on board the liner was still spanking new after her post-war refit and her 100th voyage had passed un-remarked.

To explain his routine to him Staff Captain Donald MacLean took Peter Jackson to one side and said, 'You've just got

A group photograph of staff in the hospital on board, Jean Edwards is in the front on the left. *Jean Edwards collection*

On the occasion of his retirement Captain Donald Sorrell is flanked on his left and right by Arthur Bebe and Dr. Mackay.

Below: To say farewell to Captain Sorrell some crew members line up for a scrapbook photograph. In the centre is Captain Sorrell shaking hands with Jean Edwards. On her left is 'Jonny' Johnson, Jean Woods, John Baines, Dr. Mackay and an unidentified member of the crew. On the far left of the picture is nurse Mairi Allen. *Jean Edwards collection*

your Certificate and we don't want you getting lost if there is an emergency; so, to help you find your way around the ship, you will be my representative on the midnight, 2-4-and 6 am rounds and report back to the Bridge 'Rounds Correct' at the end of each round. Don't call me at, say, 3.30 am unless there is a real emergency!' Each night, walking these rounds, meant that seventeen miles were covered and the ship's layout soon became familiar. Things such as burst pipes had to be sorted out with the source of the flood being stopped and the water baled out. Occasionally, bad weather would smash a porthole and the deadlight (the steel version of the glass port) would have to be secured over the aperture. One's way was soon found around the ship and problems were dealt with sensibly as they arose.

Whilst on night watch during the few spare moments that presented themselves Peter Jackson would practice on the magnificent Steinway piano in the early hours of the morning. He was given a spare key for this instrument on which he played his favourite Chopin and Beethoven. Unbeknown to him, Wally Adams, a fruitstoreman, would quietly enter the lounge and sit listening, discreetly, hiding behind a pillar.

Another officer who enjoyed playing was First Officer Noel Jones. Because of the many Joneses at sea he was known as 'Mendelsohn' Jones. Another Jones was known as 'Corpus' as his family had an undertaking business!

Association with passengers was forbidden and although navigating officers had their own table in the Main Restaurant they were not allowed to dine with passengers as they do now. Officers were also not allowed in the lounges unless on security patrol but they could invite passengers to their wardroom for afternoon tea.

So the *Queen Mary* carried on with her work, giving practical experience to those who wanted it, work to many who valued it (some jobs were often handed from father to son), and in return receiving love and loyalty – crew members from the *Queens* were proud of their own ship, had their own tie, formed their own clubs and were jealous of their own *Queen's* reputation. They even had their own car club badges.

With such loyalty the *Queens* would prosper.

Chapter Seven

Mary and the Movies

Born into an age when the ocean liner was the only way to travel great distances in relative safety and great comfort the 'Big Ship', the *Queen Mary*, attracted the big names. Over the years the *Queen* carried hundreds of thousands of passengers and numbered amongst these were the rich and the famous, helping to give the ship an aura of glamour. The curious public were fed with news of important arrivals of people of note by reporters who themselves were 'characters' and sometimes somewhat flamboyant: Jack Frost (who co-authored excellent biographies on the *Mary*, *Elizabeth* and *QE2*) with his straw boater and bow tie (he became a personal friend of passengers and crew alike) and Hannen Swaffer, were both commentators on the coming and goings of the famous and rich in pre- 'jet set' days. Their reports in the national newspapers were widely read with avid interest.

Politicians, sportsmen, ministers of governments and churches, musicians, royalty (including the Duke and Duchess of Windsor) and titled worthies, movie stars as well as the infamous and unfamous all travelled on the *Mary*. Household names of the day such as Montgomery of Alamein, Lord and Lady Louis Mountbatten, Sir Winston Churchill, Sir Thomas Beecham, Lord Beaverbrook, General and Mrs Eisenhower, voyaged along with perhaps not-so-well known bankers, millionaires and industrialists.

But it was the movie stars who created the greatest stir when they disembarked at or sailed from Southampton in the 1930s, 40s and 50s, times when the cinema provided a major source of entertainment with its performers often idolised.

Some of the crew became compulsive autograph hunters and many a menu, photograph or album was dedicated and signed by the famous passengers.

Sir Cedric Hardwick, sailing on the *Queen's* maiden voyage with his family, was one of the first film stars to travel on the ship. He would be followed in later years by Henry Fonda, Charlton Heston, John Mills, Victor Mature, Elizabeth Taylor, Rex Harrison and Kay Kendall, Michael Wilding, Katherine Hepburn, Richard Burton, Deborah Kerr, Robert Ryan, Johnnie Ray, Bette Davis, Robert Mitchum, Karl Malden, Claude Rains, Anna Neagle, Margaret Rutherford, Charles Boyer and many more – all of whom sailed on the *Mary* at one time or another, some of them returning time and time again to the ship they loved.

Stories abound about the stars, some humorous, some sad, some scandalous so, to accompany the reproduced photographs of a few of the film-stars who favoured the *Mary*, a tale or two would not be amiss:

After dining well in the Main Restaurant, Spencer Tracey was asked by one of the chefs if the actor would sign his autograph book. Feeling more mischievous than truthful Spencer Tracey wrote 'Thank goodness for Alka Seltzer!' before adding his signature.

The world-renowned pianist Liberace, voyaging on the *Mary*, would often play for the passengers and on one crossing one of his many sequined coats shed its shimmering embellishments. Stewardesses volunteered to sew them back on, all three thousand of them! Whilst Liberace was waiting for his jacket, two other members took the opportunity to obtain his autograph and presented him with sugar models of his piano and candelabrum.

Phil Silvers travelled on both *Queens* when he was at the height of his popularity as the scheming television Sergeant Bilko. One of the engineers was due to be introduced to Mr and Mrs Silvers and was quite nervous at the prospect. He kept on telling himself that he must say 'Mr Silvers' and not 'Mr Bilko'. When the introduction was effected he managed 'Good morning, Mr Silvers' quite well, but let himself down with 'Good morning, Mrs Bilko'!

Some of the travelling celebrities would go down aft to the crews' own pub, by tradition called 'The Pig and Whistle', and join in the crews' weekly show. Ted Heath and His Band played for them and Nancy Sinatra sang for them. Gracie Fields was a great favourite and she loved to sing for the crew and Dorothy Lamour followed in the steps of royalty by sitting amongst the crew to watch the performance.

Alec Guinness, that most talented of English actors, wrote on a photograph, taken on board, that had caught him blinking '....not really as drunk as I look!'

Phil Silvers, alias the notorious 'Sergeant Bilko', travelled on both *Queens*. *Wally Adams collection*

Joan Crawford journeyed with her two daughters and seemed to be the perfect mother – the girls even wrote 'Thank you' notes to the captain at the end of the trip. The revelations made years later by one of her daughters shocked the world.

There are stories, too, about the other passengers and these are just as interesting, just as humorous as the yarns about the people in the limelight.

Richard Burton

Gracie Fields and Rosemary Squires

Elizabeth Taylor and her parents.

Gloria Swanson

Joyce Grenfell

Charlton Heston

Alec Guiness

One such story is told by Mike Smith, who became the captain's 'Tiger' or personal steward, whilst waiting at the prestigious Captain's Table:

One of the guests at the Captain's Table was a millionairess who had risen from lowly beginnings but never forgot her Cockney background – or accent.

Quickly perusing the menu with its enormous selection of dishes the lady in question spotted the addendum at the bottom of the page informing the passengers that if they could not see what they required on the menu all they had to do was to inform their waiter and arrangements would be made to obtain what was wanted. So the wealthy woman said: "ere, Mike! I'd like fish 'n' chips wrapped up in 'The News of the World'!'

A not unreasonable request but as the ship was only a day out from New York the English Sunday newspaper posed a bit of a problem.

Undeterred, Mike Smith scoured the crews' quarters until an old, crumpled edition of the newspaper was found which, with

Liberace, shown here receiving a sugar model of his piano, was travelling home after suing a British newspaper for libellous allegations.
Wally Adams collection

Nancy Sinatra was a favourite with the crew! *Wally Adams collection*

the application of an iron, was made presentable. With great aplomb the fish and chips, wrapped in newspaper and accompanied by a huge bottle of vinegar, was presented to the delighted gourmet who proceeded to consume it with great relish.

Good service was always appreciated and as the lady left the table she tipped the resourceful waiter – with a $100 bill!

One of the most popular passengers ever to sail with the *Queen Mary* was Her Majesty Queen Elizabeth the Queen Mother. She had sailed to the United States, for a tour, on the *Queen Elizabeth* three weeks earlier and for the return trip Cunard arranged for Commodore Ivan Thompson, captain of the *Elizabeth*, to transfer his flag to the *Mary*. This was an unpopular decision with the *Mary's* crew as they felt it was a slight on their own beloved captain, Donald Sorrell.

Geoffery Marr was at this time Staff Captain of the *Mary* but he was asked to act as liaison officer between the royal party and ship and to arrange an on-board itinerary for the Queen Mother. After her energetic American tour it was thought that Her Majesty would like a restful trip. Not a bit of it! The Queen Mother wanted to see everything and meet as many as possible.

On the first night out the Queen Mother chose to dine in the Main Restaurant and the room was full to capacity for the occasion. As she entered, dressed in a gown of blue and gold, the entire assemblage rose to its feet.

The Queen loved films, and each evening Geoffery Marr would call for her as soon as the cartoons were over.

On the last night out Her Majesty held a small, sparkling dinner party in the Verandah Grill and afterwards invited her guests back to her suite. The Staff Captain thought it was merely to bid her guests 'Goodnight' but coffee and liqueurs awaited them. Geoffery Marr recited John Masefield's poem about lighthouses for Her Majesty as the *Mary* was due to pass Bishop Rock that night.

On arriving at Southampton on Tuesday evening, 23rd November, at 8.30 the Queen Mother asked to see the liner docking so Geoffery Marr escorted her to the port bridge wing where he could describe what was happening.

The Royal traveller left behind her a ship full of happy people. She had presented gifts to several of the crew – a silver crested comb for Senior Sister Moy in the surgery, a portrait in a leather frame and a silver cigarette case for Mrs Geoffery Marr; she had been, as Geoffery Marr recalls '....so very charming and gracious and made you feel so much at home.'

Stories about the celebrities who travelled on the *Mary* could fill books – and have. The *Queen* also seemed to change peoples' attitudes to one another once they were on board. Hard-line politicians softened to those of dis-similar leanings and businessmen relaxed and clinched many an important deal whilst on board.

The *Queen Mary* carried stars and made stars. She, herself, became a star of films and television shows proving that once 'on stage' she could not be 'up-staged'.

Frank Sinatra co-starred with the liner in 'Assault on a Queen', made in 1965, when she played herself. Luckily, it was the only time in her career when a U-boat got the better of her! She took on a character part in 'The Poseidon Adventure', the first and best of a spate of pseudo-disaster movies, that was based on Paul Gallico's book. In this she played the fatally unstable SS Poseidon, although mainly in model form. Parts in various 'soap' television detective series followed but she has taken to her recent screen rôles with the ease of a gentle lady in distress.

To be associated with the *Queen* in those days meant a measure, however small, of success.

Chapter Eight

The Queen Dowager

In the eleven years following their post-war refits the two *Queens* were an enormous success. Cunard, its emblem a lion holding the world in its paws, also carried the 'lions share' of the North Atlantic passenger trade. Of this share the giant sisters laid claim to a sizeable proportion. A one million peak was reached in 1957.

The *Mary* had lost the Blue Riband to the *United States* in July 1952. This liner beat the *Queen* by a comfortable margin with 35.59 knots but her maximum speed was kept a secret. She had been built on warship lines and it has since been revealed that she could achieve 40 knots! In that same year members of the *Mary's* crew were plagued by the anti-communist witch hunt that was sweeping the States. Questions and questionnaires assailed the crew each time the liner docked and many a witty answer was provided. 'What are you?' – 'I'm a commis!' – commis, pronounced 'commy', was an assistant to a waiter but sent the questioning officer into paroxysms of rage.

With their ships making money 'hand over fist' the Cunard management of the day became complacent in many ways. They ill-advisedly refused to recognise the aeroplane as a serious threat to sea-travel and also a large shore staff was built up, administering from several offices in each country of operation. Money was being made but it was also being spent almost recklessly.

However, in 1958, the problem stared Cunard in the face, for this was the year in which the number of passengers flying the Atlantic by the fast, ever-increasing jet aircraft equalled the number travelling by sea, one million to one million. By 1964 the figures showed that four million had travelled by air but in the same period Cunard's carrying capacity had fallen to 650,000. A particular voyage, November 1961, became typical of winter

The *Mary* on one of her many departures from Southampton, being waved goodbye by hundreds of well wishers.

George Norton courtesy C. English

travel with the *Mary* carrying just over 470 passengers out of her capacity of over 2,000! Crew numbers remained at the same level of over 1,000.

To help reduce costs, the summer dry-docking was omitted from 1963 onwards. These had always occurred during the *Queen's* peak season but by cutting the two annual overhauls to just one in the winter, Cunard gained the revenue from an additional summer voyage and saved the cost of the peak-season lay-up.

The *Mary* approaches the famous Manhattan skyline of New York.

Courtesy, University of Liverpool Cunard Archives

Realising that fewer passengers were travelling during the winter months Cunard decided to put the *Queens* to cruising. For the *Mary* this meant making the first cruise, in February 1963, that a Cunarder had made from Britain since 1939. During the ensuing years she cruised from Southampton to Las Palmas and from New York to Nassau and the Mediterranean. Because of her draught and breadth she could not anchor in these ports (along with many more) and she could not traverse the Suez or Panama Canals to further lucrative markets. (This has been spectacularly remedied by the *QE2*). Her lack of air-conditioning was also a great draw-back.

One cruise was chartered by the British Sunday newspaper 'News of the World' as a prize to its readers who could correctly place various features of cruising in the correct order. The ship sailed on 23rd December 1965 in a gale of force 5 to 6. By the time the *Mary* had reached the notorious Bay of Biscay this had increased to force 9. A heavy sea crashed over her and a one ton ventilating cowl was torn off its seating, crashing into a ¾ inch thick glass plate Promenade Deck window, shattering it and badly cutting a passenger who had fortunately had time to shield

his son. After Finisterre the gale subsided and the Christmas cruise was enjoyed from then on, the bad weather becoming only a half-remembered incident.

By 1966 the *Mary* was still fast, still showing her fighting spirit, when she crossed the Atlantic at 29.68 knots. That same year saw the disastrous seamens' strike that lasted for six weeks and cost Cunard nearly £4 million.

Calls at Cobh were instigated in 1967 but in spite of new ports of call, new itineraries for cruising, the *Queen Mary* was by now losing up to £8,000 a day.

A new chairman had been appointed by Cunard in 1965 and his new philosophy was intended to make the line pay, no matter how drastic or unpopular his proposals would be.

As a consequence, Captain William Laws opened a sealed envelope on board the *Queen Mary* on 8th May 1967. Contrary to what previous Cunard chairmen had said about the long-term viability of the *Queens*, Sir Basil Smallpiece announced:

'It is a matter of great regret to the Company and to me personally, as it will be to friends throughout the world, that these two fine ships, the *Queen Mary* and the *Queen Elizabeth*, must shortly come to the end of their working lives. They hold a unique position in the history of the sea, and in the affections of seafaring people everywhere. But we cannot allow our affections or our sense of history to divert us from our aim of making Cunard a thriving company and no other decision will make commercial sense.'

Top left: In appreciation of one of many missions of mercy, the *Queen Mary* received a citation from the Pentagon for rescuing the crew from a damaged US submarine.

Above: Passengers from Waterloo Station, London, to the dockside in Southampton travelled by special boat train. Here 'The Cunarder' is pulled by 'Lord Nelson' Class No. 30855 *Robert Blake.* L. Elsey

Left: A typical pose showing the giant liner alongside the Ocean Terminal, Southampton. August 1967.
John H. Bird

It was therefore decided to put the *Mary* up for sale. Cunard did not particularly want her to go for scrap but neither did they want her to be operated in competition to them.

After many bids, with many a strange suggestion as to the ultimate usage of the *Queen*, Cunard accepted a $3,450,000 offer from the City of Long Beach in California, the deal being signed on 18th August by representatives of Cunard and the corporation of Long Beach. The ship would be used as a maritime museum, conference centre and hotel.

So, after years of faithful service, the *Queen Mary* was to be pensioned off. Her initial building cost of £5 million had earned Cunard £132 million. She had sailed just over 3,790,000 miles, had carried 2,114,000 passengers and had won herself an immortal place in the affections of a nation – ask any schoolboy, even now, to name an ocean liner; his answer......?

The *Mary* left New York on 22nd September 1967 at noon amidst momentous and tearful farewells. Despite a two-day storm she arrived at Southampton on 27th September, having achieved 27.86 knots on this, her 1001st crossing, amidst a welcoming reception of fireboats, small craft and a mostly silent crowd on shore. The mood was subdued.

The *Mary's* master for her last Atlantic voyage was Captain John Treasure Jones, one of the most natural public-relations orientated captains that Cunard has ever had. He had had a varied and interesting career starting with White Star – he had been made redundant from this company as he had less than fifteen years experience with the line which would have guaranteed him continuing employment after the amalgamation with Cunard; stevedored in Liverpool; joined Cunard White Star; became a naval commander during the war after being torpedoed and commanding anti-submarine patrols and, as a commander, became Divisional Sea Transport Officer in the Dutch East Indies; re-joined Cunard after the war and joined the *Queen Mary* for the first time as Chief Officer in 1953.

His favourite ship was '...the one that I was currently Captain of,' – and it fell to him to be captain of the *Mary* during her last days at sea.

When he was asked by Cunard if he was surprised at the *Queen Mary's* forthcoming disposal, John Treasure Jones replied, 'no, I'm not surprised. I'm just surprised that you've kept her going for so long and losing so much money!'

During her ultimate crossing the *Mary* met her younger sister, the ships 'closing in' to within one mile of each other. At ten minutes past midnight on 25th September the two largest liners passed each other on the dark Atlantic, brilliantly lit and with funnels floodlit, providing an unforgettable experience to the few who braved the lateness of the hour and the wind. This last poignant meeting was over in a few minutes as the liners sped by each other at a combined speed of 60 knots.

Never again would they meet.

The last arrival of RMS *Queen Mary* at Southampton on 19th September 1967.   *R. Bruce Grice*

Chapter Nine

A Wonderful, Beautiful Toy

Ten thousand people watched the *Queen* sail from Southampton on Tuesday 31st October 1967.

The day before, the port's floating crane had lifted two red London buses onto the liner where they were secured aft on the main deck. These were going to be used to transport visitors from the centre of Long Beach to the ship once she was operational in her new home town.

The City of Long Beach in Orange County, California, had bought the *Mary* and her value quoted on her export licence (other information: *Queen Mary*; Numbers 'One'; Description of package 'One ship'; etc) was $3,450,000.

Cunard had agreed to deliver the ship and to supply the minimal crew to do so and the fuel to get there on a slow speed voyage. But the new owners did not want that alone, they wanted the delivery trip to become a cruise, in spite of the ship not having facilities for hot weather voyaging. She would also have to go via Cape Horn with its inherent dangers. So Long Beach arranged for Furgazy Travel to sell the trip as 'The Last Great Cruise' in order to recoup some of the $650,000 delivery costs. In the event 1,093 passengers paid up to $9,000 each and a profit of $125,000 was realised. 806 crew were taken on (119 deck, 98 engine and 589 catering staff) but they would be overworked and only after strong representations would overtime be paid.

On the day before sailing for Long Beach two London buses were embarked, their advertised destination Walthamstow!

Southern Evening Echo

Busy tugs take the strain as the *Mary* is eased into the stream of Southampton Water.

R. Bruce Grice

4,700 tons of fuel and 8,560 tons of fresh water for various purposes would be loaded but this would have to be replenished en-route as the *Mary* had been designed for the Atlantic route and not for the 14,559-mile journey she was about to undertake. Seven stop-overs had been arranged for the ship at ports that were capable of handling her.

HRH Queen Mary's personal standard had been taken off the ship and stored safely until it could be installed on the new *QE2*.

So, at 9.30 am on 31st October with pilot Jack Holt once more on the bridge, the Band of the Royal Marines playing 'Auld Lang Syne' on the quayside, with fourteen naval helicopters flying in anchor formation overhead and a 310 foot long pennant flying from her main mast the *Queen* left Berth 107 in a tearful farewell. Shop staff in the city climbed to the roofs of their stores to witness her passing and, as the *Mary* passed by, the *Oriana* signalled, 'Adieu, great *Queen*'. The liner replied, 'Thank you, thank you, thank you very much and good luck to you all.'

Tears ran down the face of the *Queen's* Master At Arms, 'Oh! That was a grand, grand goodbye', as crowds waved and vessels blew their sirens as the *Mary* sailed by.

Passing by Cowes for the last time the *Mary* read a signal from the exclusive Royal Yacht Squadron, 'I am sorry to say goodbye. Very best wishes.'

The passage to Lisbon, her first port of call, was rough and took about two days. In the English Channel en-route she passed *HMS Hermes*, the British aircraft carrier whose company lined the flight deck to cheer the *Queen* rousingly.

At Lisbon a stowaway, Stacy Miller, joined the ship and the next stop was Las Palmas where nearly 6,000 tons of oil fuel was taken on.

The *Queen* had to make a slow passage (which chagrined many a misunderstanding passenger) of around 20 knots. This was done to conserve fuel; she would use 1,100 tons on the North Atlantic to maintain her high speed, but this would consume the fuel up too quickly so two engines and half the boilers only were operational. As a result, only 550 tons of fuel was burnt daily.

The journey to Rio de Janeiro from Las Palmas would cover 3,540 miles and once there the *Queen* was again refuelled with 2,460 tons.

Early, on the morning of her arrival at Rio, on Monday 13th November, the death occurred, through cerebral haemorrhage caused by heat stroke, of fish cook Leonard Horsburgh, aged 56, who had been known as 'Lobster' to his friends because of his ruddy complexion.

By the time of the arrival at Rio the 'Mermaid Bar' had been reduced to using paper cups, through pilferage of glasses, and had become known as the 'Lily-cup Bar'. At the port, funds had been raised amongst the crew for a representative to go ashore to buy drinks for use on board. When the time came for the *Mary* to sail the assignment had not arrived and the purchaser was beginning to feel that he might become none too popular.

As the ship sailed a tug raced out of Rio and the *Mary* slowed as a cargo port was opened and various boxes were taken on board. These were detailed as 'Ship's stores' but were, in fact, the belated packages of 'crews' booze'!

At 11.15 am the burial at sea took place of Len Horsburgh and his body was committed to the deep. The captain had in all good faith chosen this relatively late hour for the commitment to show the passengers what a burial at sea was like. Unhappily, the crew did not see it this way and were offended when cameras clicked as the burial progressed, the passengers treating the event as an additional spectacle not on the published itinerary.

As the ship headed south the captain found it increasingly

Surrounded by craft bidding her farewell and with her 310 foot pennant billowing out from her main mast the *Queen* passes Hythe on her way to Lisbon, her first port of call. *John H. Bird*

difficult to communicate with Cunard in England, long delays frequently occurring. Eventually Cunard told Captain Treasure Jones, 'Get her there by yourself and don't try to contact us' and he was thus left to his own devices. Far from being daunted, he welcomed the enhanced responsibilities thrust upon him and said later that being in sole charge of the *Mary* was like having '...... a wonderful and beautiful toy that you had to be very careful with!'

On Sunday 19th November the *Queen* passed Cape Horn in mid-afternoon. No-one knew what the weather was going to be like but it turned out to be cloudy, clear, with a moderate north-east wind creating a slight swell. For four hours people queued and paid $1 to ride on a London bus around the Horn. The proceeds went to an orphanage in Valparaiso and certificates were given out to mark the 'Rounding'. One man dived into the swimming pool to say that he had swum around the Horn whilst another pedalled away on a bicycle in the gym!

That night, the weather blew up just to show what the Horn could really offer.

The rest of the journey up the West Coast of South America towards Valparaiso continued to be rough and she arrived at the port on 23rd November having completed the longest part of her journey, 3,895 miles.

The next stop-over was at the old sailing ship port of Callao on the 28th and then Balbao where 3,500 tons of bunkers was taken on.

A sight not often seen in the days of sailing ships. The dreaded Cape Horn as seen from the decks of the *Queen Mary*. *Captain John Treasure Jones*

Captain John Treasure Jones – with his wife behind him – hands over the ship's flags at a brief ceremony on the quayside at Long Beach on 9th December 1967. The Mayor and Deputy Mayor figurehead the City's welcoming committee. *Captain John Treasure Jones*

The Mary a few days after arrival and awaiting her complete renovation.
Roger Hardingham

Acapulco came next on 5th December and she stayed here overnight. All the crew had shore leave (save for safety parties) and, for a change, the *Queen* was fêted.

Champagne cocktail parties had been held since Valparaiso with caviar and Havana cigars being freely distributed. This was due not so much as to the party spirit prevailing on board but to US import restrictions on foodstuffs and a ban on Cuban imports.

500 miles from Long Beach a DC-9 jet met the *Queen* and,

repeating an incident on her maiden arrival in New York, bombarded the liner with flowers, most of which missed. However, the airliner's captain, A. Heimerdinger, later sent Captain Treasure Jones a framed and signed photograph of the event.

The arrival at Long Beach was nothing short of spectacular as 'Eight thousand if there was one!' boats came to meet the ship fifteen miles out in order to escort her in to her berth. The craft kept well clear of the liner as her course had been well-publicised by the authorities and her sea-lane was made into a Federal waterway with a years imprisonment or a $2,000 fine for those who infringed it.

By 11.30 am, Saturday 9th December 1967, amidst the noise and cheering of an estimated million people, the ship came alongside her berth. At 2.50 pm the passengers began to disembark and at 4 pm two stowaways were landed into the care of the FBI. (The second stowaway had boarded at Acapulco.) At a brief dockside ceremony the captain was presented with a flowered key to the city and he handed over the Cunard houseflag.

The crew were flown home almost immediately as their 72 hour visas would not allow them much time for sight seeing.

On the following Monday a slightly delayed ceremony took place on board, aft of the Verandah Grill. A telephone linked the ship with Cunard in London and Lord Mancroft informed Captain Treasure Jones that the '...... Long Beach cheque was a good one and had not bounced!' As the American flag was raised to take the place of the British ensign the Captain felt a lump in his throat, realising that it was all over.

Left: Part of one of the badly rusted funnels is lifted ashore. Cufflinks made from chips of paint were produced and these showed, in strata form, the career of the *Queen*. *Right:* Dry-docked at Long Beach after her delivery voyage from Southampton, the *Queen* has her bottom cleaned and propellers removed at the start of her lengthy renovation.
Illustrated London News

So ended the long and eventful career of the Royal Mail Ship *Queen Mary*. She was to become, after a planned $8 million (later raised slightly to $100 million plus!) conversion, a building and is now known as the Hotel *Queen Mary* and advertised as '81,000 tons of fun!' She has since been joined by Howard Hughes' giant flying boat, the *Spruce Goose*, and has also changed hands with her ownership passing to the Wrather Corporation.

But she still remains a monument to the ingenuity and craft of British shipbuilding, a memorial to thousands of soldiers who travelled in her during time of war and a symbol of peace between two great nations who have so much in common. May she long enjoy her sunny retirement.

The *Queen* is still remembered and her memory cherished. To mark the occasion of the 50th anniversary of her maiden voyage her grand descendant the *Queen Elizabeth 2* undertook a '*Queen Mary* Anniversary Voyage' from Southampton on Saturday 3rd May, 1986. The Queen Mother took lunch on board the liner and met many of the *Queen Mary's* passengers and crew who were on board for the maiden voyage. The food from the 1936 menus was served during the voyage and Captain John Treasure Jones gave talks to a new generation of traveller.

As a final post-script, the choosing of the *Queen Mary's* name has for years been a matter of debate and a story that has hitherto been repudiated by many as 'folk-lore' seems to have been vindicated. In a letter to the author Frank Braynard, that renowned maritime historian and author of New Jersey and curator of many a maritime museum, wrote recently:

'My father was part of a small delegation from Cunard Line that called on King George V to ask his permission to name their new superliner after Queen Victoria......' So began a piece of fascinating dinner conversation recently. The person talking was a lovely woman with sparkling eyes and cordial manner. I jumped to attention because I knew the story she was going to tell. In fact, I had used it 40 years before in my first book 'Lives of the Liners' (1947) and ever since I had smarted at word that my story was bunkem. Cunard denied it, point blank. It was just made up. I listened with eagerness.

'You know all Cunard ships have had names that ended with '....ia' and Victoria would have been a perfect choice, being well suited for the world's largest ship then being built by the company,' she continued.

'My father opened the conversation with His Majesty by saying something to the effect that Cunard wished to name its new superliner 'after England's greatest queen. Queen Mary, who was with her husband on this occasion, smiled and said, 'I would be delighted.'

And so one of the greatest names of all maritime history was selected. The *Queen Mary* remains to this day perhaps the best known of modern liners. And I felt most gratified because the lady telling the story was none other than the daughter of Sir Ashley Sparks, Chairman of the Cunard Steamship Company in America!'

Rolls Royces transport passengers, who were on the maiden voyage of the *Queen Mary*, to the QE2 on 3rd May 1986. *David F. Hutchings*

Acknowledgements

In the researching of this brief history of the *Queen Mary* many people were either interviewed for first-hand information or else offered assistance by the loan of cherished photographs or mementoes of the ship.

I would especially like to thank Commodores Donald MacLean and Geoffery Marr and Captain John Treasure Jones for their invaluable assistance, the former two amplifying many instances contained within their most readable autobiographies. Thanks also to Captain Peter Jackson for relating his experiences as a Junior Third Officer on the *Mary*, Edwin Praine (a young commis-waiter at the time of the maiden voyage), Wally Adams for the use of his photographs of the stars who travelled on the ship and Harley Crossley, the excellent marine artist from Sherborne in Dorset, for permission to use his work.

Amongst others to whom I am indebted are: Rod Baker, Len Betts, Norman Blundell, Frank O. Braynard, Bob Bruce Grice, Jean Edwards, David Easton, Mr C. English, Miss Freda Ferguson, Miss Elsie Greenman, Keith Gould, John Havers, Jack Horner, Judith Jacobs, Susan Leatherbarrow, Bill Mitchell, Sylvia Mitchem, Bert Moody, Mike Smith, Sandy Vinter, Peter Walters and Jean Woods – and also the wives of the interviewees who kindly gave me tea!

Amongst the organisations I would single out Nigel Overton of the Southampton Maritime Museums, Peter Ashton of the Southern Evening Echo and representatives of the National Maritime Museum, Imperial War Museum, The University of Liverpool (for the Cunard Archives), The Illustrated London News and the Cunard Line (Public Relations).

My sincere thanks also go to Roger Hardingham of Kingfisher Railway Productions for his enthusiasm and assistance and for the honour he did me in inviting me to write this Golden Anniversary tribute to the greatest of all ocean liners.

A fitting endpiece: the two *Queens* meet in the new docks at Southampton after the war.
Southern Evening Echo

Bibliography

Benstead, C R – 'Atlantic Ferry' Methuen & Co. Ltd. 1936
Bisset, Commodore Sir James – 'Commodore' Angus & Robertson Ltd. 1961
Bonsor, Noel – 'North Atlantic Seaway Vol. 1' David and Charles 1975
Braynard, Frank O – 'Lives of the Liners' Cornell Maritime Press 1947
Coleman, Terry – 'The Liners' Penguin Books Ltd. 1976
Cunard Line booklets – 'Art on RMS Queen Mary', 'The Stateliest Ship Now In Being', 'Launch of the Queen Mary', 'The Cunarders' 1969
Grattidge, Captain Harry – 'Captain of the Queens' Olbourne Press 1956
Harding, Steve – 'Grey Ghost – the RMS Queen Mary At War' Pictorial Histories Publishing Co. Ltd. Montana 1982
Hughes, Tom – 'The Blue Riband of the Atlantic' Patrick Stephens Ltd. 1973
Hyde, Francis E – 'Cunard and the North Atlantic 1840-1973' The Macmillan Press Ltd. 1975
Kludas, Arnold – 'Great Passenger Ships of the World, Vol. 3, 1924-1935' Patrick Stephens Ltd. 1976
Lacey, Robert – 'The Queens' Sedgwick & Jackson 1973
MacGuire, Joseph B – 'The Sea My Surgery' William Heineman Ltd. 1975

MacLean, Commodore Donald – 'Queens Company' Hutchinson 1965
Marr, Commodore Geoffrey – 'The Queens and I' Adlard Coles Ltd. 1973
Miller, William and Hutchings, David – 'Transatlantic Liners At War – the Story of the Queens' David & Charles 1985
Ocean Liners of the Past – 'The Cunard White Star Quadruple Screw Liner Queen Mary' Bonanza Books, New York
Potter, Neil and Frost, Jack – 'The Queen Mary' Harrap 1961
'Railways, Ships and Aeroplanes' – (various contributors) Odhams Press Ltd.
'Shipbuilding and Shipping Record'
Southampton Corporation – 'The Queens', 'RMS Queen Mary – the Log of Voyage No. 516', Harvey Barton – St Stephens Publications
Steamship Historical Society of America – 'The Stateliest Ship'
Time Life Books – 'The Great Liners' Time Life Books 1978
Tute, Warren – 'Atlantic Conquest' Cassell 1962
Wheeler, Harold (editor) – 'The Wonderful Story of the Sea' Odhams Press Ltd.
Winchester, Clarence – 'Shipping Wonders of the World' Fleetway House Ltd. 1957